Easy

Origami

Decorations

An Augmented Reality Crafting Experience

by Christopher Harbo

CAPSTONE PRESS

a capstone imprint

First Facts are published by Capstone Press,
1710 Roe Crest Drive, North Mankato, Minnesota 56003
www.mycapstone.com

Library of Congress Cataloging-in-Publication Data
Names: Harbo, Christopher L., author.
Title: Easy origami decorations : an augmented reality
    crafting experience / by Christopher Harbo.
Description: North Mankato, Minnesota : Capstone Press,
    2017. | Series: First facts. Origami crafting 4D | Includes
    bibliographical references. | Audience: Ages 6–9. |
    Audience: Grades K to 3.
Identifiers: LCCN 2016041210 | ISBN 9781515735854
    (library binding) | ISBN 9781515735908 (ebook (pdf))
Subjects: LCSH: Origami—Juvenile literature.
Classification: LCC TT872.5 .H3733 2017 |
    DDC 736/.982—dc23
LC record available at https://lccn.loc.gov/2016041210

Summary: Provides photo-illustrated instructions for making
five origami models and three craft projects. Also includes
embedded video links for online instructional tutorials that
can be accessed with the Capstone 4D app.

Editorial Credits
Sarah Bennett, designer; Laura Manthe, production specialist

The author thanks Rachel Walwood for designing and
creating all of the origami craft projects in this book.

Photo Credits
Photographs and design elements by Capstone Studio: Karon
Dubke. Line drawings by Capstone: Sandra D'Antonio.
Additional design elements: Shutterstock: Ammak, Lena
Bukovsky

Printed in the United States of America.
010077S17

Table of Contents

A Decorator's Dream Come True

The simplest origami models look amazing by themselves. But pair them with a few craft supplies and a good imagination, and something magical happens. A paper butterfly becomes a beautiful magnet for your school locker. Origami cubes become glowing paper lanterns that will draw "oohs" and "ahhs" from your friends. Each model has endless possibilities — the only limit is what you can dream up!

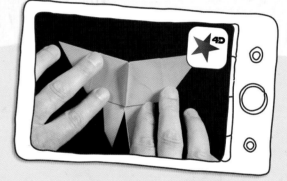

Download the Capstone 4D App!

Videos for every fold and craft are now at your fingertips with the Capstone 4D app.

To download the Capstone 4D app:
• Search in the Apple App Store or Google Play for "Capstone 4D"
• Click *Install* (Android) or *Get*, then *Install* (Apple)
• Open the application
• Scan any page with this icon

You can also access the additional resources on the web at **www.capstone4D.com** using the password **fold.decorate**

Materials

Origami is great for crafting because the materials don't cost much. Below are the basic supplies you'll use to complete the projects in this book.

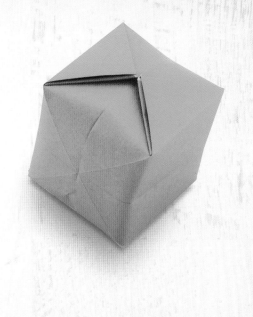

origami paper

colored card stock

scissors

craft glue

ribbon

string

glue sticks

beads

wire

LED lights

candy

markers

yarn

magnets

Terms and Techniques

Folding paper is easier when you understand basic origami folding terms and symbols. Practice the folds below before trying the models in this book.

Valley folds are represented by a dashed line. One side of the paper is folded against the other like a book.

Mountain folds are represented by a dashed and dotted line. The paper is folded sharply behind the model.

Squash folds are formed by lifting one edge of a pocket. The pocket gets folded again so the spine gets flattened. The existing fold lines become new edges.

Inside reverse folds are made by opening a pocket slightly. Then you fold the model inside itself along the fold lines or existing creases.

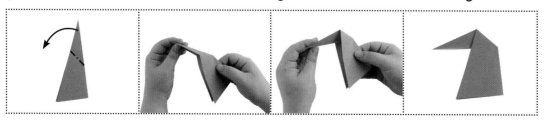

Outside reverse folds are made by opening a pocket slightly. Then you fold the model outside itself along the fold lines or existing creases.

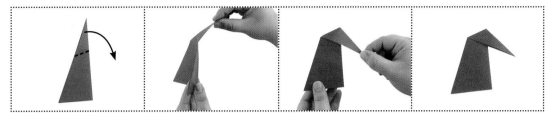

Rabbit ear folds are formed by bringing two edges of a point together using existing fold lines. The new point is folded to one side.

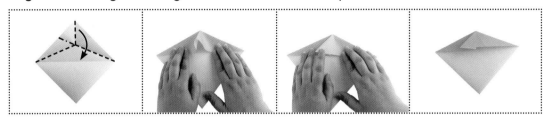

Pleat folds are made by using both a mountain fold and a valley fold.

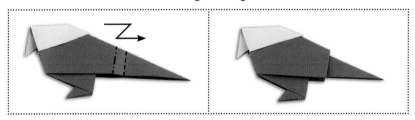

Symbols

Fold the paper in the direction of the arrow.	Fold the paper and then unfold it.	Fold the paper behind.
Turn the paper over, or rotate the paper.	Pleat the paper by reverse folding twice.	Inflate the model by blowing air into it.

Butterfly

Butterflies come in countless colors and patterns. Take a hint from nature. Let your imagination run wild when picking colorful paper for this model.

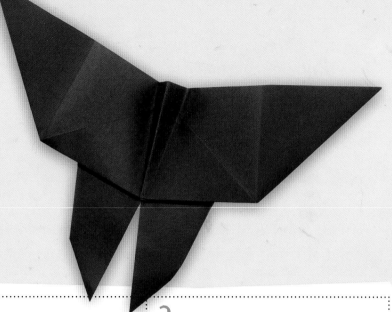

1 Valley fold edge to edge in both directions and unfold.

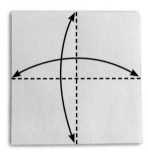

2 Valley fold corner to corner in both directions and unfold.

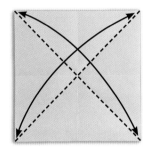

3 Valley fold the corners to the center.

4 Turn the model over.

5 Valley fold the corners to the center and unfold. Turn the model over.

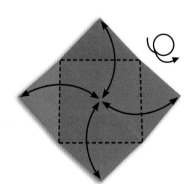

6 Unfold the paper completely.

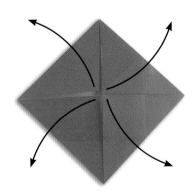

7 Valley fold the edges to the center.

8 Squash fold the corners using the existing creases.

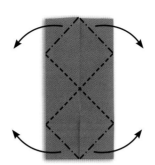

9 Mountain fold the model in half.

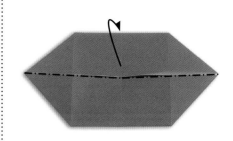

10 Valley fold the top flaps to the center.

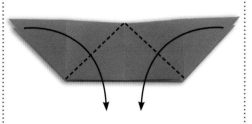

11 Valley fold the corners of the top flaps.

12 Valley fold the model in half.

13 Valley fold the top wing at a slight angle. Repeat behind.

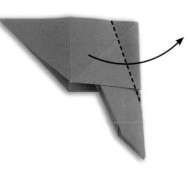

14 Unfold the model halfway.

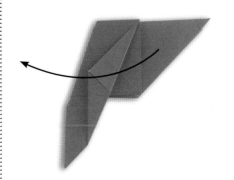

15 Finished butterfly.

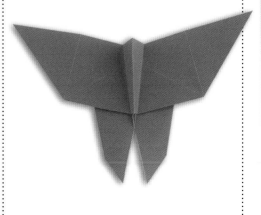

Butterfly Magnet

Turn origami butterflies into magnets in no time flat! This quick and easy craft is the perfect decoration for refrigerators and school lockers.

What You Need

craft glue

2 1-inch (2.5-centimeter) long pieces of stiff string or wire

origami butterfly

6 4-inch (10.2-cm) long pieces of yarn

small magnet

*fold the butterfly from a 6-inch (15-cm) square

What You Do

1 Glue the stiff string or wire to the back of the butterfly's head to make antennae.

2 Glue the yarn to the butterfly's tail. Divide the yarn evenly between both sides of the tail.

3 Glue the small magnet to the center of the butterfly's back.

4 Once the glue dries, stick your butterfly magnet to a refrigerator, locker, or other metal surface.

Cube

Making an origami cube takes more than just nimble fingers. You'll inflate this model like a balloon with a puff of air.

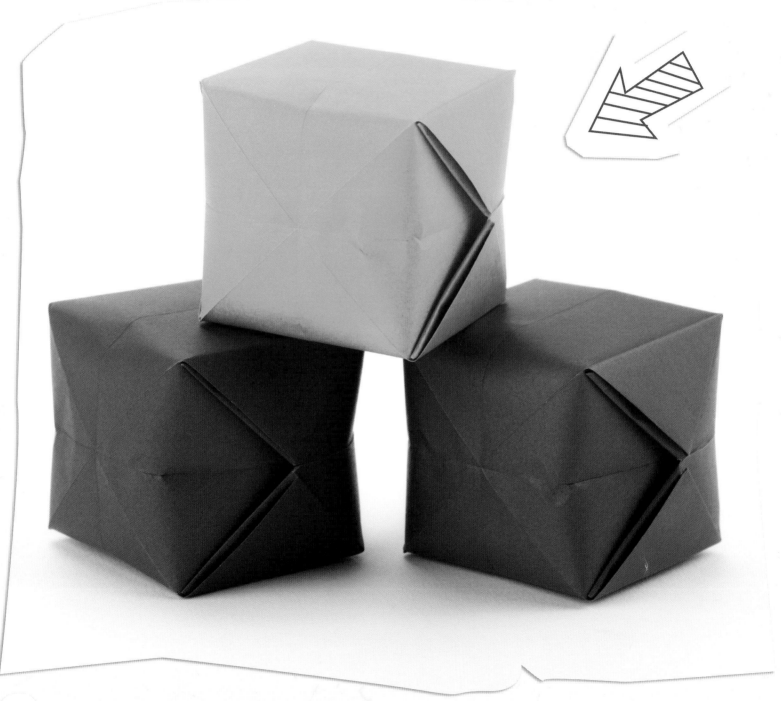

1 Valley fold edge to edge in both directions and unfold. Turn the paper over.

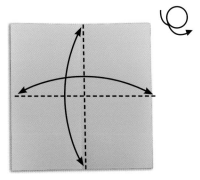

2 Valley fold corner to corner in both directions and unfold.

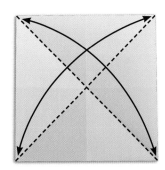

3 Squash fold the paper using the existing creases.

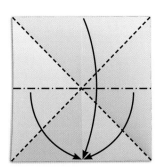

4 Valley fold the top flaps to the point. Repeat behind.

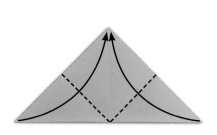

5 Valley fold the top flaps to the center. Repeat behind.

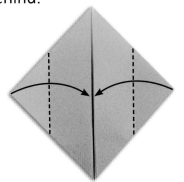

6 Valley fold the top flaps to the center. Repeat behind.

7 Valley fold and tuck the small triangles into the pockets. Repeat behind.

8 Spread the model's layers slightly and blow into the bottom hole to inflate.

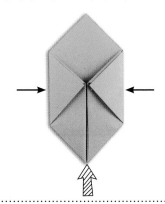

9 Finished cube.

Paper Lanterns

Add pizzazz to any party with homemade paper lanterns. Just place a few origami cubes on a string of LED lights, and you're good to glow!

What You Need

scissors

spool of string

string of LED lights

beads

spool of ribbon

origami cubes

*fold all origami cubes from 6-inch (15-cm) squares

What You Do

1 Cut a length of string slightly longer than the LED lights. Lay it parallel to the string of lights.

2 Slide beads onto the string and space them evenly along its length.

3 Tie one end of the string to one end of the lights.

4 Wrap the string around the light string. Work from the knot tied in step 3 to the end of the light string. Be sure to keep the beads evenly spaced as you go. Then tie off the loose end of the string.

5 Cut short strips of ribbon and tie them all along the light string. These ribbons will help hold the string and beads in place.

6 Push each LED light into the hole of an origami cube.

7 Plug in the light string and enjoy your glowing paper lanterns.

Swan

This simple swan is more than just a pretty bird. Its wings can open to hold your tiniest treasures.

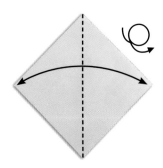

1 Valley fold corner to corner and unfold. Turn the paper over.

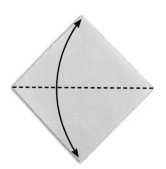

2 Valley fold corner to corner and unfold.

3 Valley fold the edges to the center and unfold.

4 Rabbit ear fold on the creases made in step 3. At the same time, mountain fold the center crease.

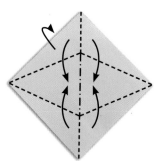

5 Valley fold both points. Allow the points to land about halfway between the corners and the left point.

6 Valley fold the points.

7 Mountain fold the model in half.

8 Pull the neck up and flatten.

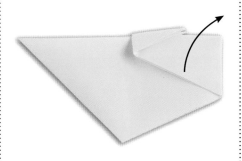

9 Pull the head up and flatten.

10 Mountain fold the bottom point. Repeat behind.

11 Finished swan.

Tulip

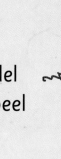

Breathe life into this model with a puff of air. Then peel its petals to see how an origami tulip is born!

1 Valley fold edge to edge in both directions and unfold. Turn the paper over.

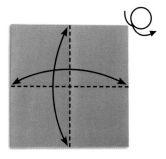

2 Valley fold corner to corner in both directions and unfold.

3 Squash fold the paper using the existing creases.

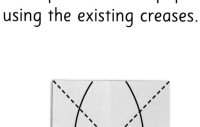

4 Valley fold the top flaps. Repeat behind.

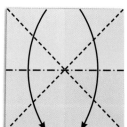

5 Valley fold the top flap. Repeat behind.

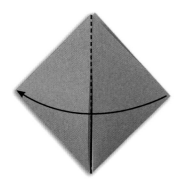

6 Valley fold the corner of the top flap just past the center crease.

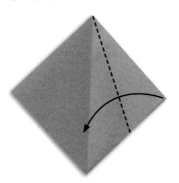

7 Repeat step 6 on the left flap. Tuck the corner into the pocket.

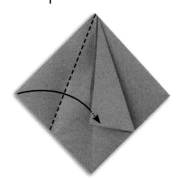

8 Turn the model over.

9 Repeat steps 6 and 7 with the remaining flaps.

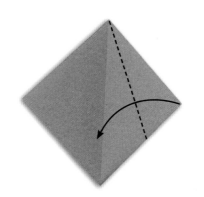

10 Valley fold the bottom point and unfold.

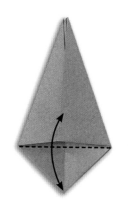

11 Gently blow into the hole in the bottom point to inflate the model.

12 Gently peel down the petals like you would peel a banana.

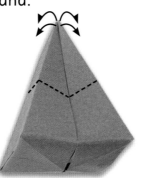

13 Finished tulip.

Stem

Every origami flower looks better with a stem. Make your paper blossoms shine on this simple model.

1 Valley fold corner to corner in both directions and unfold.

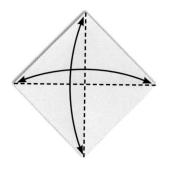

2 Valley fold the edges to the center.

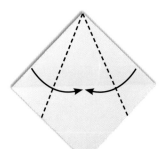

3 Valley fold the edges to the center.

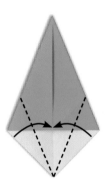

4 Valley fold the edges to the center.

5 Valley fold point to point.

6 Valley fold the model in half.

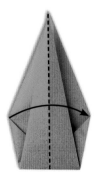

7 Outside reverse fold the point.

8 Finished stem.

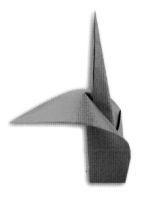

Springtime Centerpiece

Decorate your table with a touch of spring. This clever centerpiece is blooming with style. And the candy-filled swans will be a hit with all of your guests.

What You Need

2 4.5- by 5-inch (11- by 12.5-cm) pieces of green card stock

scissors

5 small diamond-shaped pieces of card stock

marker

12-inch (30-cm) long piece of string

glue stick

2 origami stems

2 origami tulips

2 origami swans

assorted candy

*fold all origami models from 6-inch (15-cm) squares

What You Do

1 Fold a narrow flap on a long edge of each piece of green card stock. Stand the cards up on their flaps.

2 Cut long, narrow slits in the upright portion of both cards. Nest the cards to form a patch of grass. Place the grass in the center of your table.

3 Fold the five diamond-shaped card stock pieces in half to form flags.

4 Write one letter on each flag to spell the word "PARTY."

5 Hang each flag on the string in order. Glue them in place. Set aside.

6 Cut a notch near the tip of each origami stem. Make the notch on the straight edge of the stem directly above the leaf.

7 Thread the ends of the string through the holes created by the notches. Tie knots in the string to keep the ends from pulling out of the stems.

8 Place one stem on each side of the grass. Drape the flags over the grass in a way that pleases you.

9 Slide an origami tulip onto the tip of each stem.

10 Fill the wings of each origami swan with candy. Place anywhere near the tulips and grass to complete your centerpiece.

Read More

Bolte, Mari. *Paper Presents You Can Make and Share.* Sleepover Girls Crafts. North Mankato, Minn.: Capstone Press, 2016.

Lim, Annalees. *Origami Crafts.* 10-Minute Crafts. New York: Windmill Books, 2016.

Sanderson, Jennifer, and Jessica Moon. *Paper Decorations.* Origami and Papercraft. Mankato, Minn.: Arcturus Publishing, 2015.

Song, Sok. *Origami Outfits: A Foldable Fashion Guide.* Fashion Origami. North Mankato, Minn.: Capstone Press, 2016.

Internet Sites

FactHound offers a safe, fun way to find Internet sites related to this book. All of the sites on FactHound have been researched by our staff.

Here's all you do:
Visit *www.facthound.com*
Type in this code: 9781515735854

Super-cool stuff! Check out projects, games and lots more at **www.capstonekids.com**